Mastering The Mental Side Of Coaching

Hemispheric Kinesiology

Ernest Solivan

Mastering The Mental Side Of Coaching

Mastering The Mental Side Of Coaching

Copyright © 2017
All Rights Reserved

ISBN: 978-0-6151-7234-7

Mastering The Mental Side Of Coaching

"If winning isn't so important why do they keep score."
      Vince Lombardi

Mastering The Mental Side Of Coaching

Table of Contents

Introduction - 7

The Mind - 11

The Conscious Mind - 15

The Subconscious Mind - 17

The Critical Factor - 23

Critical Factor Bypass - 27

The Brain - 31

The Left Hemisphere - 35

The Right Hemisphere - 39

Muscle Testing - 45

Stress - 51

Synthesizing Events - 55

The Egocentric Stage - 59

Dissociation - 67

The HK Performance Trigger - 69

Winning - 73

Programming In The HK Performance Trigger - 77

Mastering The Mental Side Of Coaching

Table of Contents

HK Journaling - 81

How To Use The HK Performance Trigger - 85

Mind Mastery For Coaching - 89

Setting Goals - 93

Your Athlete's Mechanics - 97

Communicating With Your Athletes - 101

Using Imagination During Practice - 105

Conclusion - 109

Introduction

Mastering The Mental Side Of Coaching

You are coaching a football game and it's the 4th quarter with 30 seconds on the clock. Your team has first and goal. You are losing by 3 points. Do you go for the touchdown, or kick a field goal? Or, you're in the 7th inning, and your pitcher has been pitching pretty well up to this point, and you have a 1 run lead. It's two outs with runners on 1st and 2nd. Your pitcher has a 3-2 count on the batter. Do you pull the pitcher or leave him in?

These are decisions made by coaches everywhere that dramatically influence the outcome of the contest. Mastering The Mental Side of Coaching is a book that will provide you with a perspective that may help explain why some coaches make the decisions that help them win the contest, and some coaches make decisions that cause them to lose the contest.

With the advent of quantum physics, science must now acknowledge that there are things that happen below our level of conscious awareness that dramatically affects your coaching. Mastering The Mental Side Of Coaching is a book that explains why you may be struggling with your coaching (no matter what the sport), and how you can change struggle to success using a remarkable technology called Hemispheric Kinesiology (HK).

This is a book about HK and how it can help you become a winning coach. HK is a muscle testing success technology that allows me to access, isolate and change undesirable subconsciously stored information preventing coaches from coaching their best.

HK's most salient characteristic is that it offers a very credible, rational and viable explanation as to why coaches experience problems during competition and provides a remedy that will allow them to coach to the best of your ability.

There is an old saying that you cannot teach an old dog new tricks. This is a testament to how difficult change is for just about everyone. There are basically three elements necessary to create change in your life.

They are Sensation, Perception and Conception. Sensation is the capacity to experience; Perception is the capacity to be aware of what you are experiencing; and Conception is taking action to begin the process of change, or it can also represent a rebirthing into some new experience. HK works on the simple premise that if it stresses you to coach, you are not going to do it well.

Please set aside your prejudices, beliefs and judgments and do your best to keep an open mind. HK is a little different twist on psychology. This discipline was created with the intention of allowing you to help yourself facilitate and accelerate positive changes that will immeasurably improve the quality of your coaching, as well as your personal life. And, isn't that what we are all looking for?

Mastering The Mental Side Of Coaching

The Mind

When you set a goal to do something, one of two things will happen. You will either succeed or fail. What determines your success or failure is the information contained in your Mind. This stored information is the information you will use while attempting to accomplish your goal.

If the information in your Mind supports you in successfully completing your goal, the accomplishment of your goal will be easy and almost effortless. However, if the information in your Mind does not support you in successfully accomplishing your goal, the accomplishment of your goal will be very difficult and require a tremendous amount of effort.

The Mind is generally thought to be the seat of consciousness. It is made up of every aspect of our being. There are many philosophies that view the Mind in a way that has created numerous fragments, i.e., the spiritual mind, the emotional mind, the etheric mind, etc. I found all these subdivisions of the Mind to be very confusing.

In HK I rely upon the very old axiomatic metaphysical concept known as "cause and effect." Several of the theories that support cause and effect are, "for every action there is an equal and opposite reaction;" "water seeks it own level;" and "what goes around, comes around."

When we deal with the Mind we are dealing with something we cannot see. Although I cannot see a coach's Mind, I can see the experiences that Mind is creating. For instance, if I am working with a coach who can only win 10% of his games, I must assume that he has information stored in his Mind to support him in winning only 10% of his games, or he would be doing something else.

It is important to note that your Mind supports you in everything you do. If you can only win 10% of your games, your Mind is supporting you, and it is doing so based upon information it has stored in its memory banks relating to your win/loss percentages. Your physical body is merely acting out (i.e., 10% win/loss average) based upon this stored information, and it does it automatically.

To understand cause and effect, you must first understand that before anything physically happens in your life, it must first start as a thought. So, if you want to change the undesirable experiences you are creating, you must change the thoughts that are responsible for creating those undesirable experiences.

For example, the information stored in the coach's Mind is the "cause" (10% win/loss average), while the experience he is creating (10% win/loss average) is the "effect." The coach is creating this experience because his physical body is responding by corresponding to information stored in his Mind.

The intention of this program is to provide coaches with a resource that will allow them to create positive change and help them become winning coaches during competition. Before I explain how this is accomplished, it is important to establish a context and foundation whereby all the contributing factors to this performance phenomenon may be examined and understood.

Let's first examine your Mind. The Mind has two parts. The Conscious Mind, and the Subconscious Mind.

Mastering The Mental Side Of Coaching

The Conscious Mind

The Conscious Mind is known as the "knower" because it has the ability to be aware of itself. It has the capacity to be aware of what it is thinking and feeling in the normal waking state. It also has the ability to know what it is doing and why. One of the major functions of the Conscious Mind is its use of volition. Volition is defined as, "the act of using the will; exercise of the will as in deciding what to do; a conscious or deliberate decision of choice thus made."

You are where you are in your coaching life right now as a direct result of the choices you have made using the volitional part of your Conscious Mind. The Conscious Mind provides us with short-term memory and can only focus on one thing at a time. The Conscious Mind uses the five senses; sight, hearing, smell, taste and touch, to collect information which allows it to experience awareness.

The Conscious Mind uses this collected information to formulate your self-image, your prejudices, and your belief system. The most important function of the Conscious Mind is that it exercises its volitional capabilities by allowing us to set goals. The information collected by the Conscious Mind will influence the formulation and successful completion of the goals you set throughout your coaching life.

So, what happens when the Conscious Mind, using its volition, decides to engage in some particular activity like coaching? Well, it types out a mental memo of instructions and sends it to the Subconscious Mind.

The Subconscious Mind

When you engage in a particular activity, such as coaching, it is the responsibility of your Conscious Mind to decide the nature of the activity. Your Conscious Mind will send instructions to your Subconscious Mind, "Send me all the information you have relating to coaching."

If the information accessed from your Subconscious Mind relating to coaching is supportive in nature, you will perform the activity easily and efficiently. However, if the information accessed from your Subconscious Mind is not supportive or contradicts the goal set by your Conscious Mind, your coaching activity will become very difficult and require a tremendous amount of effort.

The Subconscious Mind is a part of the Mind known as the "doer" because it merely does what it is programmed to do. Unlike the Conscious Mind, the Subconscious Mind does not have the capacity to exercise volition or choice, it simply "does."

The Subconscious Mind acts out through the physical body and uses information it has stored in its memory banks relating to the particular activity (coaching). This "acting out" is done instantaneously and automatically. This stored information arrived into the Subconscious Mind through the Conscious Mind using the five senses (sight, hearing, smell, taste, and touch).

To more fully understand this acting out phenomenon, remember when you were a child learning how to tie your shoes? At first it required a tremendous amount of time and concentration. Now, you do it without consciously thinking because it has become a subconscious act. The same thing happens when you engage in coaching related activity. Your physical body automatically acts out base upon information obtained from your Subconscious Mind relating to everything from your self-image to your win/loss percentage ratio.

The Subconscious Mind is a storage facility for all information that enters through the Conscious Mind. The one important feature to note about the Subconscious Mind is that when it is storing information it is impersonal. It doesn't say, "I am not going to store this experience because it was a bad experience." IT STORES EVERYTHING!

The Subconscious Mind also provides you with long-term memory, and is where your belief system is housed. If you have information stored that you can only win 10% of the games in which you coach, your physical body will reciprocate by only allowing you to win 10% of the games you coach. It has no other choice but to use the information available. Your Subconscious Mind will continue to do it until you change the information.

Additionally, the Subconscious Mind does not have a sense of humor and cannot distinguish between something real or imagined. If you don't believe me, try telling someone who has a fear of heights that they have nothing to be afraid of. You can clearly see how powerful our beliefs are, and that they have a tremendous influence, both positive and negative, over the decisions we make throughout our lives.

The Subconscious Mind can be likened to the hard drive of your computer with one notable exception. When using a computer, you have the option of saving or erasing the information on your screen.

Every piece of information that enters the Subconscious Mind is stored for future use.

Your Conscious Mind will eventually use this subconsciously stored information when it engages in an activity that corresponds to the information in storage. The Subconscious Mind will provide the Conscious Mind with whatever information it has available. The information can be supportive or non-supportive in nature.

When subconsciously accessed information is non-supportive, the physical body will manifest stress. For instance, let's say you set a goal at the beginning of the season to win 90% of the games you coach, and the information you have stored subconsciously is that you are only capable of winning 10%. Your physical body will immediately manifest stress.

Your Subconscious Mind is basically telling your Conscious Mind, "I do not have the information stored to support you in winning 90% of the games you coach, however, I do have information stored to support you in winning 10%." The end result, you are going to win 10% of the games you coach.

WHENEVER THERE IS CONFLICT BETWEEN THE CONSCIOUS MIND AND THE SUBCONCIOUS MIND, THAT CONFLICT WILL ALWAYS MANIFEST IN THE PHYSICAL BODY AS STRESS!

It's as if the Conscious Mind and the Subconscious Mind are not on the same page. When stress is present in the physical body, it will always weaken the body. It is when your physical body is in this weakened or stressed state during competition that you will call a play with disastrous results.

It's as if your physical body goes on red alert because the information in the Conscious Mind (90% of games won) does not match the information accessed from the Subconscious Mind (10% of games won). The Subconscious Mind, acting out through the physical body, will do everything in its power to sabotage any victories over 10%.

There is a very integral component of the Mind that gets involved when the Conscious and the Subconscious Mind interact. It is known to as the Critical Factor.

Mastering The Mental Side Of Coaching

The Critical Factor

After information enters the Conscious Mind, it is reviewed prior to storage in the Subconscious Mind. The responsibility for this task belongs to a component of the Mind known as the Critical Factor. The Critical Factor literally criticizes or reviews information that comes into conscious awareness.

After its review, the Critical Factor must make a decision regarding the disposition of the information. The Critical Factor has two options. It can either store the information, or reject it. Everyone knows that the color of the sky is blue, but suppose I told you that the color of the sky was red.

When that statement enters your Conscious Mind, your Critical Factor will stop it momentarily and says something to the effect, "Let me check the information I have in subconscious storage relating to the color of the sky." The Critical Factor checks and discovers that the information stored in the Subconscious Mind indicates that the color of the sky is blue. The Critical Factor proceeds to reject the statement, "The sky is red."

Let's also assume that the coach that can only win 10% of his games sets a goal to win 90% of his games. His Conscious Mind will send instructions to his Subconscious Mind, "Send me all the information you have stored relating to winning 90% of the games I coach."

His Critical Factor will stop this information before it hits the Subconscious Mind and say something to the effect, "Let's see what kind of information we have in subconscious storage relating to winning 90% of the games you coach."

Mastering The Mental Side Of Coaching

The Critical Factor checks and discovers that the information stored indicates that the coach is only capable of winning 10% of the games he coaches, and proceeds to reject the statement. It's as if the Critical Factor instructs the coach's Subconscious Mind to go on "red alert" and proceeds to sabotage any attempt this coach may make to win more than 10% of his game.

Imagine the Critical Factor as a guard, and that it is guarding all information coming into and leaving the Mind. How do you change this information? How do you change subconsciously stored information preventing you from becoming a winning coach? In order to change subconsciously stored information, we must achieve Critical Factor Bypass.

Mastering The Mental Side Of Coaching

Mastering The Mental Side Of Coaching

Critical Factor Bypass

Critical Factor Bypass occurs when new information is allowed to bypass the Critical Factor of the Mind in an effort to change old information stored in the Subconscious Mind. HK can achieve Critical Factor Bypass, which enables you to literally change subconsciously stored information.

Using HK to achieve Critical Factor Bypass allows you to accelerate change for the coaches who experience it. In order to more fully understand Critical Factor Bypass, we must first look to the advertising industry.

On many occasions advertising agencies will send sales copy to a psychologist, and ask, "Will this copy achieve Critical Factor Bypass for our product or service?" The ad agencies know that if they can achieve Critical Factor Bypass on anyone who hears or sees their commercials, their chances of selling their product or service are greatly enhanced.

They carefully choose the people who star in these commercials, carefully choose the wording, and carefully choose the scenarios. How can they motivate someone to buy their product or service? One way to do it is using fear in the form of authority figures. It cannot be done blatantly. It must be subtle.

Have you ever noticed that in many commercials, ad agencies will use policemen, judges, doctors, or firemen. All these professions represent authority figures and the ad agencies know that when a policeman tells you to do something, you normally do it without question. You do what you are told because the policeman was able to achieve Critical Factor Bypass.

Another very subtle tactic ad agencies will use to create Critical Factor Bypass is race and gender. I once saw a print ad that contained a Caucasian, an African-American, an Asian, an older gentleman, an older woman, a young man, and a young woman. They covered a lot of bases with that ad.

Companies will also use celebrities to achieve critical factor bypass. Many people love and respect celebrities and will be influenced by what they say. It's interesting that whenever a celebrity, for instance, has a negative encounter with the law, the company will immediately pull the ad.

Sometimes the ad agencies will appeal to your emotions. I am certain you have seen the Michelin Tire commercial with a baby sitting in a tire. That commercial has been running for years. This particular commercial has been successful because the ad agency was able to achieve Critical Factor Bypass by using the baby to appeal to the emotions of the viewer. Michelin must have sold a lot of tires, or they would not have continued to use this very effective commercial which had run for years.

Some of the other tactics used by ad agencies are humor, sex and money. In fact, the next time you view or hear a commercial advertisement, ask yourself, "What are they doing in this commercial to achieve Critical Factor Bypass?" I will explain in a later chapter how we are able to achieve Critical Factor Bypass using HK so that the 10% winning coach can become a 90% winning coach.

For now, we have examined the nuances of the Mind to include the Conscious Mind, the Subconscious Mind, the Critical Factor, and Critical Factor Bypass.

Mastering The Mental Side Of Coaching

The Mind must act out through the physical body and it does this using your brain.

The Brain

Although the Mind is the decision maker, it is the brain's responsibility to physically carry out those instructions. The brain is a part of the Central Nervous System composed of approximately 10 billion nerve cells. Each cell is linked to one another, and together they are responsible for the control of all functions in the physical body. The brain disseminates these instructions throughout the physical body using information provided by the Mind in the form of electrical impulses via your nervous system.

The brain is an organ consisting of three major components. The Left Hemisphere, The Right Hemisphere and the Corpus Callosum. Although these three components are integral, they each have very specific and different functions, and two of these components can function independently should the need arise. The Left Hemisphere of the brain controls the right side of the physical body, while the Right Hemisphere controls the left side.

We need only look at a stroke victim to understand this phenomenon. Notice that in the majority of the cases only one side of the body is paralyzed. That's because the hemisphere of the brain on the opposite side of the affected area was so severely damaged during the stroke that it manifested as paralysis.

The corresponding side of the subject's physical body is not receiving electrical impulses (information) from the damaged hemisphere resulting in partial or total paralysis. There are degrees of dysfunction between the brain and the physical body, and that total paralysis represents the extreme.

Since the Left and Right Hemispheres of the brain can function independently and have their own responsibilities, they need some way to communicate. This is accomplished using the Corpus Callosum. The Corpus Callosum is a band of nerve fibers that connect the Left and Right Hemispheres of the brain. The hemispheres share and exchange information (electrical impulses) that will eventually be disseminated to the physical body.

What I realized in my research in working with athletes and coaches was that the hemispheres of the brain have a tendency to weaken or switch off. When one hemisphere is switched off, the opposite hemisphere will dominate.

For instance, if a coach's Left Hemisphere is switched off, his Right Hemisphere will dominate whatever activity he may be involved in, and vice versa. The hemispheres of the brain are continually influenced by and are reacting to, stimuli in a coach's immediate external environment.

The brain does basically three things. It processes (learns), stores, and disseminates information. What kind of information? That would be any and all information relating to pictures, sounds, fragrances, culinary data, and touch. All three of the major components of the brain come into play when the brain is exercising these functions. Let's first examine the Left Hemisphere of the brain.

Mastering The Mental Side Of Coaching

The Left Hemisphere

When the Left Hemisphere of the brain processes (learns) information, it only understands words, language and numbers. That's because the Left Hemisphere processes information sequentially, or one piece at a time. The Left Hemisphere is one-dimensional, and can only focus on one thing at a time. The Left Hemisphere controls the right side of your physical body and it accomplishes this by sending information in the form of electrical impulses.

When the Left Hemisphere of the brain weakens or switches off, during the processing or learning stage, it's as if a short circuit occurs in the electrical field in your physical body, and the incoming information never reaches the hemisphere of the brain that is switched off. Incoming information will only store in the hemisphere that is switched on.

For instance, if your Right Hemisphere is switched off while your brain is learning, the incoming information will store in your Left Hemisphere. Now, because there was no information stored in your Right Hemisphere, when it's time for your brain to disseminate the information to you at some point in the future, you will only receive information from your Left Hemisphere. It's as if you are only getting half the information.

When the Left Hemisphere of the brain stores information, it will only store sequential information such as words, language and numbers. It will store information that is logical and organized. In other words, the information stored in the Left Hemisphere must be structured.

When the brain disseminates information to the physical body, the Left and Right Hemispheres deal with different and specific information. The Left Hemisphere of the brain provides the physical body with the following information, attributes and qualities:

Logic, action, decision making, critical, one-dimensional, mechanical, compulsive, doubt, cautious, judgmental, hard working, limitation, shame, rational, stoic, organization, reasoning, rules, hard, cold, specificity, structure, boundaries, rigidity, opinionated, intense, impersonal, unfeeling, introverted, controlled, predictable, restricted, precise, serious, conservative, quiet, intolerant, auditory, scientific, temporal (the now), fearful and finite.

When you engage in an activity and the Right Hemisphere of your brain is weak or switched off, your physical body is only receiving information, or a majority of the information, from your Left Hemisphere. This causes you to become left-brain dominant while you are engaged in that particular activity. This anomaly results in you exhibiting one or more of the personality traits listed above.

For example, a left-brain dominant individual is introverted, dresses very conservatively, and is very structured. This brain imbalance causes them to do it to excess. I believe this switching off anomaly is one reason that science speculates that we only use 10% of our brain. Now let's examine the Right Hemisphere of the brain.

The Right Hemisphere

When the Right Hemisphere of the brain processes information, it only understands movement and pictures. That's because the Right Hemisphere is spatial and can process information collectively rather than sequentially. This collectiveness allows it to process large amounts of information at one time. It can only process non-sequential information.

For instance, if you were looking at a picture of a landscape with your Left Hemisphere, you would have to look at every piece of the picture individually because the Left Hemisphere processes information sequentially. You cannot see the whole picture if you are only looking at one piece. The collective capabilities of the Right Hemisphere allows you to see the whole picture, while the Left Hemisphere provides you with the capacity to structure the collective information in the form of discernible images.

When we examine this phenomenon during the learning stage of our development, we can clearly see how the hemispheres of the brain influence how we learn. Let's look at an elementary school student named Harold. He is learning to read the sentence, "See Jack jump." If Harold had the Right Hemisphere of his brain weak or switched off while reading this sentence, his Left Hemisphere would dominate.

Now, keeping in mind that the Left Hemisphere processes information sequentially, Harold's Left Hemisphere will know and understand the words <u>see</u>, <u>Jack</u>, and <u>jump</u> individually. However, because his Right Hemisphere is weak or switched off, he will have difficulty achieving total comprehension. In order for that to happen, he would have to send the information from his Left Hemisphere, via the corpus callosum, to the Right Hemisphere, and request additional information such as a visual of a boy jumping. With both hemispheres of his brain participating in the learning process, Harold will achieve total comprehension, no matter what he is learning.

When the brain disseminates information to the physical body, the Right and Left Hemispheres deal with different and specific information. The Right Hemisphere of the brain provides the physical body with the following information, attributes and qualities:

Feelings, emotions, relaxation, beliefs, creativity, flexibility, physical movement, tolerance, visualization, artistic, spatial, self-esteem, forgiveness, no boundaries, unstructured, generalizations, procrastination, compassion, optimism, passivity, funny, unreasonable, loud, expressive, foolish, passion, charming, intuition, love, uncontrollable, multi-dimensional, imagination, addictions, lazy, laid back, open-minded, unorganized and infinite.

When the Left Hemisphere of your brain is weak or switched off, the Right Hemisphere will dominate your activities, from your decision making to your personality. Since your physical body is only receiving information from the Right Hemisphere of your brain, you will exhibit one or more of the above listed personality traits and attributes, and the brain imbalance will cause you to exhibit them to excess.

Think of the time, as a basketball coach, that you became so upset while arguing with an official because of a bad call that you were ejected from the game. It is during these times when the Right

Hemisphere of your brain was dominating your thinking. With your Left Hemisphere switched off, there was nothing to balance your thinking or actions.

The objective in HK is to help you switch on both hemispheres of your brain in relationship to a thought, statement or action. Having both hemispheres of your brain switched on insures that you will have access to information such as judgment, analysis and structure (Left Hemisphere), as well as creativity, imagination and intuition (Right Hemisphere). With both hemispheres of your brain providing your physical body with information, you will experience total balance in the coaching decisions you make during competition.

A great analogy for explaining hemispheric balance is water. The Right Hemisphere can be likened to boiling hot water, while the Left Hemisphere is ice-cold water. By themselves, their temperatures are very uncomfortable. However, when you mix them together, you get a warm, comfortable and balanced temperature. When both hemispheres of your brain are switched on, you enter a mental space that athletes refer to as "The Zone."

Another salient difference between the hemispheres worthy of note is that the Left Hemisphere deals with "old" information, while the Right Hemisphere deals with "new" information. This influences how the hemispheres of your brain will handle a specific task, including coaching. Let's assume that you have just purchased something that requires assembly.

The Left Hemisphere of your brain will approach the task by saying something like, "Where are the instructions to this thing (?); I can't put this together without the directions!" Remember that because the Left Hemisphere is using "old" information, it is basically saying, "Show me the way some else did it, then I can do it."

Conversely, the Right Hemisphere will approach that same task by saying, "Hey, even if we don't have the instructions, let's put it together anyway." That's because the Right Hemisphere is providing the physical body with "new" information in the form of "creativity," and will figure it out eventually. The Right Hemisphere will risk (no instructions), while the Left Hemisphere will tend to play it safe (must have instructions).

Let's assume you are the football coach in the 4th quarter who is losing by 3 points, first and goal and must decide whether to kick a field goal or go for the touchdown, and you call your last time out. If you are a left brain dominant coach (right hemisphere switched off), you will have a tendency to play it safe. You kick the field goal. If you are right brain dominant (left hemisphere switched off), you will go for the touchdown.

When you can coach with both hemispheres of your brain strong or switched on, you will achieve a level of coaching that most coaches just dream of. With access to structure, judgment and organization (Left Hemisphere), and creativity, intuition and imagination (Right Hemisphere), every decision you make supports your team in winning the game.

The key to becoming a winning coach, and this is very important, is to remain calm and relaxed during competition because when you are calm and relaxed, your brain functions at maximum capacity. Especially during pressure situations - you will make decisions that will help you to win the contest

When I do private sessions with coaches and athletes using HK, it is imperative that I know what activity is taking place in the physical body in relationship to a statement, thought or action. This is accomplished using Muscle Testing.

Muscle Testing

There are three vital pieces of information that muscle testing allows me to obtain in relationship to a statement, thought or action. First, muscle testing allows me to determine whether the physical body is weak or strong.

Secondly, muscle testing allows me to determine the condition of the hemispheres of the brain in relationship to a statement, thought or action. Thirdly, muscle testing allows me to post test and validate that the stress has been cleared from the physical body.

Muscle testing is a technique that has been widely used in the alternative health field for years and has been used in a variety of applications. I use muscle testing to determine whether stress is present in your physical body relating to a statement, thought or action.

Since the physical body is merely acting out based upon information contained in your Subconscious Mind, muscle testing allows me to tap into that subconsciously stored information.

In his book "Switching On," Dr. Paul Dennison defines muscle testing as:

> "Muscle testing is the art of isolating and testing one muscle at a time in order to determine if it is 'weak' or 'strong' relative to the strength of the individual being tested."

There are forty-two muscle groups in the physical body. In Hemispheric Kinesiology, I muscle test the deltoid muscle. The deltoid is the larger triangular muscle of the shoulder, which raises the arm away from the side. If you held your right arm straight out from your side, parallel to the ground, and lifted your arm upward from that point, it is the deltoid muscle that allows you to execute that movement.

When I muscle test someone I will ask them to:

1. Stand with weight evenly distributed on both feet;
2. I have the subject hold his left or right arm straight out or parallel to the ground;
3. I face the subject standing in front of the outstretched arm;
4. I ask the subject to look straight ahead and extend the fingers of his outstretched arm so that they are parallel to the ground;
5. I place my left hand on the subject's left shoulder for support;
6. I place my right hand, using only two fingers (index and middle fingers) on top of the subject's outstretched arm between the elbow and wrist;
7. The subject is now ready to be muscle tested;
8. I will ask the subject to resist upwards slightly, towards the sky, while I apply about 2 ounces of pressure downward towards the ground. This allows both the subject and I to get a feel for the muscle test.

The key to muscle testing effectively is 2-2-2. Use two fingers, apply two ounces of pressure, and hold for two seconds. There are two possible responses to a muscle test. Strong, or weak.

A strong muscle test indicates that my downward pressing motion was unable to budge the subject's arm. A strong muscle test also indicates that there was no stress present in the subject's physical body relating to the statement, thought or action for which I muscle tested.

A weak muscle test indicates that the subject was unable to resist my downward pressure, and could not hold his arm parallel to the ground. A weak muscle test is evidence that stress was present in the subject's physical body relating to the statement, thought or action for which I muscle tested.

What does a strong vs a weak muscle test tell me, if anything? Well, if I had had a coach make the statement, "I consistently win 90% of the games I coach," the strong muscle test signifies that the coach's physical body would totally support him in winning 90% of the games he coaches. The absence of stress in the coach's physical body indicates that there is information stored in his Subconscious Mind that would support him in winning 90% of his games.

On the other hand, had the coach muscle tested weak to the statement relating to a 90% winning percentage, the weak muscle test indicates the presence of stress in his physical body relating to the statement. It basically stressed the coach to say, "I consistently win 90% of the games I coach."

The weak muscle test tells me that the information stored in the coach's Subconscious Mind would not support him in winning 90% of his games. A weak muscle test is the physical body's way of saying, "I am not doing that because I do not have information stored in my memory banks to support the activity, or that the information I have stored contradicts whatever it is you want to do (90% winning percentage)."

The second piece of information I can obtain using muscle testing is the condition of the Right or Left Hemispheres of the brain in relationship to a statement, thought or action. For instance, when checking the condition of the Left Hemisphere, I merely touch the left side of the coach's head and muscle test.

If I record a strong muscle test, the hemisphere is switched on. If I record a weak muscle test, the Left Hemisphere is switched off. I would do likewise to check the condition of the Right Hemisphere.

Checking the hemispheres of the brain allows me to determine how the subject would function while engaged in the activity for which we are muscle testing. For example, if I muscle tested you for the goal of winning 90% of your games, and you had your Left Hemisphere switched on and your Right Hemisphere switched off, your Left Hemisphere would dominate your approach to the goal.

You would exhibit the personality traits and attributes listed under the Left Hemisphere of the brain. You will try to use "old" information. For instance, what did I do last week to win 90% of my games; what did I do the week before; Etc. It's as if you are walking through a mental revolving door.

You keep creating the same experience (10% winning percentage). Without the participation of your Right

Hemisphere you would be lacking information such as intuition, creativity and imagination. The end result - 10% winning percentage.

Thirdly, and most importantly, muscle testing allows me to validate, through post testing, that the stress relating to the subject matter has been cleared from the coach's physical body. If I have you say "I consistently win 90% of the games I coach," and you muscle test weak, and then have you say it again, and you muscle test strong, something obviously changed in your physical body and the way it reacted to the statement.

In HK, muscle testing allows me access a coach's Subconscious Mind. If subconsciously stored information is to be changed, it must be done subconsciously. Muscle testing allows me to inferentially (indirectly) access information from a coach's Subconscious Mind using his physical body. That's because the Mind and the physical body are integral and mirror each other. What affects the Mind affects the physical body.

When the physical body is in a weakened state, it is engaged in a sabotage state. Muscle testing allows me to interpret the language used by the physical body to communicate this sabotage state, and that language is stress.

Stress

Taber's Cyclopedic Medical Dictionary defines stress as, "...the result produced when a structure, system or organism is acted upon by forces that disrupt equilibrium or produce strain...the term denotes the physical and psychological forces that are experienced by individuals." Stress has an absolutely pervasive effect on the physical body, and the prolonged presence of stress in the body can manifest pathologically (disease).

When stress is present in the physical body, it creates a myriad of physiological changes. Some of the more salient physical reactions to stress are:

* Increase in the rate and force of heartbeat;
* A rise in systolic blood pressure;
* Sweating of the palms and hands;
* Dilation of the pupils;
* Decreased digestion;
* Blood distribution from less to more active organs;
* Increased blood glucose (hyperglycemia);
* Etc;

Can you imagine having to make a decision at a crucial point in the game with all this activity going on in your body? When stress is present in the physical body, it interrupts the electrical signals between the brain and muscles causing the body to weaken. It also disrupts your thought processes. When your body is in this weakened state it is attempting to sabotage your activity.

When your body is in this weakened state during a game you will make a judgment call at a crucial point in the game that will adversely affect the outcome. This sabotaging phenomenon is so subtle that you will be totally unaware that you are doing it because it is all happening subjectively or subconsciously. That is to say it is happening below your level of conscious awareness.

The presence of stress in a coach's physical body adversely affects him mentally by weakening or switching off one or both hemispheres of his brain. We have already discussed the ramifications of this switching off anomaly. When stress is present in a coach's physical body, something is motivating his body to manifest stress. That something is a synthesizing event.

Synthesizing Events

A synthesizing event is created when the emotions from a traumatic experience actually synthesizes (comes together) with the information as it is being stored in the Subconscious Mind. This synthesized information remains stored and dormant in the Subconscious Mind until the Conscious Mind engages in some activity relative to the information or event.

Once the Conscious Mind accesses this synthesized information, it will manifest in a coach's physical body as stress. One of the best analogies I have ever heard in describing, synthesizing events is to imagine that you have just purchased a brand new boat. The hull of this boat is clean and spotless. As you travel on water, barnacles will attach themselves to the hull.

The more barnacles that attach to the hull, the slower the boat will travel, until the boat accumulates so many barnacles it stops all together. Synthesizing events are like barnacles that have attached themselves to the hulls of our lives. If you accumulate enough barnacles they may manifest as a nervous breakdown, or some chronic illness.

The barnacle analogy is likened to mental baggage that people carry around with them for years, and it adversely affects every aspect of their lives. When you accumulate too much mental baggage you will more than likely have to go on some form of medication (anti-depressants, etc) just to make it through the day.

What's responsible for creating synthesizing events? Trauma! Webster's defines trauma as, "1. A bodily injury or shock; 2. An emotional shock, often having lasting psychic effects." As you can clearly see, trauma can be experienced both physically and mentally, and can range from mild to severe. The physical trauma from dislocating a shoulder during competition, for example, will heal with time.

However, the mental (emotional) trauma from the injury may stay in an athlete's physical body for years. How about this scenario? You are a basketball coach coaching a championship game with a 1-point lead and 2 seconds left on the clock, and a player on the other team throws a Hail Mary ball and it goes in and your team loses. The resulting emotional trauma from that loss stored in your Subconscious Mind as a synthesizing event and may adversely affect your coaching for years.

There are two types of synthesizing events. The initial synthesizing event, and the subsequent synthesizing event. The following analogy explains. Suppose you had a fear of heights. There was a first time you experienced that fear and it is referred to as the initial synthesizing event because it was the first time the synthesizing dynamics came into play relating to the subject matter.

That synthesized information is stored in your Subconscious Mind, and will remain dormant until you go near a high place again. Once this happens, the Conscious Mind sends instructions to the Subconscious Mind, "Send me all the information you have stored relating to being near a high place."

The stored information from the first experience comes up, and since an emotion has synthesized with the information, it comes up as well. Your first reaction is, "Let's get away from this ledge!" The second experience created a subsequent synthesizing event.

Once you have left harm's way and are in a safe place, the initial synthesizing event is once again stored in your Subconscious Mind, and the subsequent synthesizing event is stored for the first time. Now you have two subconsciously stored pieces of information (or experiences) to support your fear of heights, and so on.

Imagine an onion. Its center represents the kind of coach you have the potential to become. Over the years you have accumulated layers of mental blockages (synthesizing events) preventing you from realizing that potential.

If you don't get rid of them at some point your onion will continue to grow and you will carry these blockages with you from competition to competition. In order to access the center of your onion (your true potential), the layers of mental blockages must be peeled away, and that is exactly what HK and this program will help you do.

Please remember that it is not what you are doing, but where you are doing it. For instance, if I were to take a 12" wide plank and connect two buildings 5 feet off the ground and ask you to walk across it. No problem. If I moved that same plank up to the 30th floor and asked you to walk across it I would surely get a different response. It is not what you are doing, but where you are doing it.

It is my belief that 95% of all synthesizing events are stored in your Subconscious Mind during a period in your childhood development known as the Egocentric Stage.

The Egocentric Stage

There is a period in your childhood known as the egocentric stage, and it occurs between conception and 7 to 8 years of age. It was during this stage in your development when most of the synthesizing events were stored in your Subconscious Mind.

Webster's defines egocentricity as, "Regarding the self or the individual as the center of all things; Having little or no regard for interests or feelings other than one's own; Self-centered." The egocentric child is so self-centered that the first thought they have when something goes wrong in their lives is, "What did I do wrong?"

If you ask a three-year-old boy if he has a brother, he will answer yes. If you ask that same three-year-old boy if his brother has a brother, he will answer no. That's because the egocentric child cannot objectify his experience, he can only experience.

It's as if he cannot see himself. The reason for this phenomenon is that the egocentric child's Mind does not possess a critical factor. Remember that the critical factor allows your Mind to accept or reject incoming information passing through your Conscious Mind.

Without the capacity to criticize incoming information, the egocentric child's Subconscious Mind stores everything! At age 7 or 8 the child's critical factor starts kicking in. During the child's teen years, it is operating at full capacity because teenagers know everything and adults know nothing. After the teen years, our criticalness starts reversing and by middle age, most of us experience a softening of our attitudes and come to realize that criticism was all a waste of good energy to begin with.

The absence of the critical factor also denies the egocentric child the capacity to rationalize. You cannot rationalize with someone who is incapable of objectifying his experiences. Some of the other anomalies associated with the egocentric child:

* Absolutize – You either love me or you hate me;
* Personalize - Takes everything personally;
* Idealize their role models – If dad says I'm stupid, it must be true;
* Self-blame – What did I do wrong;
* Shame – There must be something wrong with me;

Children have very limited resources when dealing with trauma. The only way they know how to deal with trauma is to block it out. They accomplish this by switching off one or both hemispheres of their brains depending on the severity of the trauma. This switching off will influence the decisions they make for the rest of their lives.

In the 1980's John Bradshaw brought to light much information relating to dysfunctional families. In a dysfunctional family, the members are simply not getting their needs met. But, what kind of a family environment would produce a functional child or adult? The following quote is from a book titled Trauma and Recovery by Dr. Judith Herman:

"The developing child's positive sense of self depends upon a caretaker's benign use of power. When a parent, who is so

> much more powerful than a child, nevertheless shows some regard for that child's individuality and dignity, that child feels valued and respected; he develops self-esteem. He also develops autonomy, that is, a sense of his own separateness within a relationship. He learns to control and regulate his own bodily functions and to form and express his own point of view."

Wouldn't it have been nice to have been raised in this environment? The truth is that 99% of all families are dysfunctional. This dysfunction leaves most children who experience it filled with shame and doubt. Dr. Herman continues:

> "Shame is a response to helplessness, the violation of bodily integrity, and the indignity suffered in the eyes of another person. Doubt reflects the inability to maintain one's own separate point of view while remaining in connection with others. In the aftermath of traumatic events, survivors doubt both others and themselves."

If you show a child respect, he learns to respect himself and others. If a child is shown disrespect, it traumatizes him and creates a synthesizing event. As that child is creating a self-image, the synthesizing event will no doubt play a significant role in determining how that child will perceive himself. The switching off of the hemispheres will cause the child to become either left brained or right brained dominant.

Here is an extraordinary example of how things we learn about ourselves during the egocentric stage of our development stay with us the rest of our lives. One day a teacher asked her students to list the names of the other students in the room on two sheets of paper, leaving a space between each name. Then she told them to think of the nicest thing they could say about each of their classmates and write it down. It took the remainder of the class period to finish their assignment, and as the students left the room, each one handed in the papers.

That Saturday, the teacher wrote down the name of each student on a separate sheet of paper, and listed what everyone else had said about that individual. On Monday she gave each student his or her list. Before long, the entire class was smiling. 'Really?' she heard whispered. "I never knew that I meant anything to anyone!" and, "I didn't know others liked me so much," were most of the comments.

No one ever mentioned those papers in class again. She never knew if the students discussed them after class or with their parents, but it didn't matter. The exercise had accomplished its purpose. The students were happy with themselves and one another. That group of students moved on.

Several years later, one of the students was killed in Viet Nam and his teacher attended the funeral of that special student. She had never seen a serviceman in a military coffin before. He looked so handsome, so mature. The church was packed with his friends. One by one those who loved him took a last walk by the coffin. The teacher was the last one to bless the coffin.

As she stood there, one of the soldiers who acted as pallbearer came up to her. "Were you Mark's math teacher?" he asked. She nodded, "Yes." Then he said, "Mark talked about you a lot." After the funeral, most of Mark's former classmates went together to a luncheon. Mark's mother and father were there, obviously waiting to speak with his teacher. "We want to show you something," his father said, taking a wallet out of his pocket. "They found this on Mark when he was killed. We thought you might recognize it."

Opening the billfold, he carefully removed two worn pieces of notebook paper that had obviously been taped, folded and refolded many times. The teacher knew without looking that the papers were the ones on which she had listed all the good things each of Mark's classmates had said about him. 'Thank you so much for doing that," Mark's mother said, "'As you can see, Mark treasured it."

All of Mark's former classmates started to gather around. Charlie smiled rather sheepishly and said, "I still have my list. It's in the top drawer of my desk at home." Chuck's wife said, "Chuck asked me to put his in our wedding album." "I have mine too," Marilyn said, "It's in my diary." Then Vicki, another classmate, reached into her pocketbook, took out her wallet and showed her worn and frazzled list to the group. "I carry this with me at all times," Vicki said and without batting an eyelash, she continued, "I think we all saved our lists."

If you tell a 6 year old he isn't good enough, he has no way of stopping that information. It goes right into subconscious storage and will be used at some point in his future to create his self-image. If you treat that same 6 years with respect and tell him he is loved and cherished he will, likewise, store the information subconsciously and it will have a profound positive impact on his self-image, and he will carry it with him for the rest of his life.

Many children start their athletic careers playing some

kind of organized sport during the egocentric stage of their development. If you are a coach, please be ever mindful of what to tell these children whenever you interact with them. Because they respect you, they will believe everything you tell them.

Sometimes the trauma is so severe that it causes both hemispheres of the brain to weaken or switch off. This creates a condition known as "Dissociation."

Dissociation

As I had mentioned earlier, children do not have a lot of options when dealing with trauma. Children deal with it by blocking it out. They accomplish this by switching off one of both hemispheres of their brains depending upon the severity of the trauma. When both hemispheres of the brain switch off it creates a condition known as dissociation.

Dissociation occurs when specific mental functions become separated (or dissociated) from the mainstream of consciousness and, as a consequence, are lost to the individual's awareness and voluntary control. When a coach, for instance, dissociates during the decision making process in a game, he does not have access to creativity or intuition (Right Hemisphere switched off), nor is there structure to his thinking (Left Hemisphere switched off).

It's as if you are totally disconnected from your body. There is a way to help coaches keep both hemispheres of their brains switched on during competition and it involves achieving Critical Factor Bypass. This is accomplished with the use of the HK Performance Trigger.

Mastering The Mental Side Of Coaching

The HK Performance Trigger

We now know that when a coach experiences a traumatic encounter (losing a close game), the emotions from that trauma will synthesize with the information stored in his Subconscious Mind and adversely affect his future coaching. In order to clear the synthesizing event(s), a desynthesis must occur. In order to neutralize the synthesizing event, I employ the HK Performance Trigger.

The HK Performance Trigger creates a medium to facilitate the release of trauma and all associated emotions connected to that trauma from a coach's Subconscious Mind manifesting as stress in his physical body.

In other words, the intention of the HK Performance Trigger is to sever the emotional trauma from the information stored in a coach's Subconscious Mind creating the stress in his physical body. It works because "energy follows intention."

In other words, the HK Performance Trigger is used to create Critical Factor Bypass so that you may change the subconsciously stored information preventing you from becoming a coach capable of winning 90% of the games he coaches. Every time you use the HK Performance Trigger you are changing information on a subconscious level.

Or, to put it another way, you are peeling the onion. Your objective is to get to the center of the onion because that is where you will find your true potential to become a winning coach. The more you do something the better you get at it. So, the more you use the HK Performance Trigger, the stronger and more effective it becomes.

The HK Performance Trigger was designed to help you peel away the psychological blockages preventing you from coaching your best during competition. Now, let's show you how to use HK to clear these blockages.

The first part of this book was intended to provide you with a context that would help you understand why you are not coaching up to your potential. The second part will show you how to use HK so that you may gain the maximum benefit. First, let's examine the word winning.

Mastering The Mental Side Of Coaching

Winning

Before you can understand what it takes to become a winning coach it is important to look at the etymology of the word win. The word win comes from the Greek word "winnen" which literally means "to struggle or contend." However, when we look at Webster's definition of win, we get a different meaning.

Webster's defines win as, "to gain a victory; be victorious; triumph; to finish in first place in a race, contest, etc." What makes a winning coach? Well, there must be information stored in his belief system/Subconscious Mind to support him in winning. Webster's defines belief as, "something believed; opinion, conviction; confidence in the truth or existence of something not immediately susceptible to rigorous proof."

What kinds of beliefs, opinions, or convictions do you have about yourself relating to winning? What form of rigorous proof can you give me that you are a winner? In order to create a winning belief system, you must first become aware of the information you have stored in your belief system/Subconscious Mind relating to winning. Self-awareness is crucial to effecting positive change. You cannot change something you are not aware of.

If your thoughts create your experiences, you must first change your thoughts relating to winning. Once this happens, your experience will change. The intention of this program is to helping you become a winning coach.

Please don't think I am intimating that you are incompetent as a coach, but because everything is relative, there is always room for improvement. If you

Mastering The Mental Side Of Coaching

are a football coach who only eight games last year, you could have won 9, or 10, or 11, etc.

What you are about to learn in the following pages will help you become more calm, focused and relaxed during competition, and help provide you with the mental clarity necessary to become a winning coach. You will be shown step by step:

1. How to program in the HK Performance Trigger;
2. How to use the HK Performance Trigger;
3. How to do the HK Journaling exercise;
4. How to use the Mind Mastery For Coaching program;"
5. The importance of setting goals.

Let's first show you how to program in the HK Performance Trigger.

Mastering The Mental Side Of Coaching

Mastering The Mental Side Of Coaching

Programming In The HK Performance Trigger

There are three steps to programming in the HK Performance Trigger:

Step #1: Read the following statement aloud:

"I, (state your name), now accept and integrate into my morphic field the HK Trigger which is stating, thinking or hearing the word 'relax' and touching the thumb and index fingers of both hands, to immediately and permanently collapse to the zero point of my morphic field and neutralize all information manifesting as stress in every cell, organ and tissue of my physical body as well as my morphic field, and to 'switch on' the left and right hemispheres of my brain as well as my corpus callosum so that all three components function as one allowing me to always remain in present time, and to activate that part of my morphic field that supports and allows me to experience and be open to receive more wealth, health, happiness, peace, joy, prosperity, safety and security in my life, and all other attributes I may require to help me experience the lifestyle of my choosing, to help me successfully accomplish all my goals, and to improve the quality of my life relating to every statement, thought and action I experience, layers one through infinity, and I will never interfere with the physical manifestation of all my goals, needs and desires, and every time I activate my HK Trigger it will become ten times more powerful, and to help me switch on that part of my mind that allows me to experience sound logic, good judgment, superb analysis, powerful creativity, insightful intuition, and profound empathy, and all other attributes I may require to help me always coach my best during competition and become a winning coach; help my team win every game I coach; and help me successfully accomplish all my personal and coaching related goals, relating to every statement, thought and action I experience, layers one through infinity."

Step #2: Say the word "relax" and touch the thumb and index fingers of both hands, then release and open your fingers.

Step #3: Read the statement in Step #1 again. Remember to read it aloud so that you involve as many of your senses as possible. The HK Performance Trigger, which is stating or thinking the word "relax" and touching the thumb and index fingers of both hands, is now programmed into your Subconscious Mind.

The HK Performance Trigger is intended to help you stay calm, relaxed, and focused. When you can remain calm and relaxed while coaching during competition your brain functions at maximum capacity. This will provide you with the mental clarity necessary to help you create a strategy that will support your team in winning the game. This ultimately results in more consistency in your thought processes and the decisions you make during the game will dramatically enhance your team's chances of winning the game.

If the presence of stress in your physical body indicates that you are in a sabotage mode, then the intention of the HK Performance Trigger is to get you in a calm and relaxed state of mind during competition. When you can remain calm and relaxed while coaching your games that is when you coach your best.

During this peak mental state, both your Conscious and Subconscious Mind are on the same page. When your Conscious Mind decides to do XYZ, your

Subconscious Mind will support you in doing it, and you will do it well.

The reason the HK Performance Trigger is so effective is because "energy follows intention." Remember that the more you use the trigger, the stronger it becomes. There is an excellent process we use in HK to extract information from your Subconscious Mind. It is called HK Journaling.

HK Journaling

Remember that one of the limitations of the Conscious Mind is that it can only focus on one thing at a time. If you are not winning as many games as you would like, there is usually more than one thing responsible for the problem. HK Journaling allows you to bring up those problems, or the negative experiences you had during your game, one at a time, and in order of their priority.

HK Journaling entails the use of open-ended statements to access subconsciously stored information manifesting as problems during competition. Grab a pencil and a blank piece of paper and draw a line down the center of the page. At the top of the left side of the page write the word Negative. At the top of the right side of the page write the word Positive.

Using open-ended statements list the negative things that occurred for you during your game on the left side of the page. For instance, let's assume that you are a football coach and your team just lost an important conference game. Here is how you would document this information.

1. One of the negative things that occurred during my last game was: We lost the game by 3 points;

2. The second negative thing that occurred during my last game was: On 4th and goal I decided to go for it instead of kicking a field goal;

3. The third negative thing that occurred during my last game was: Etc.

After you have finished documenting all the negative things that occurred for you during your game, go to the top of the right side of the page and document all the positive things that occurred for you.

1. One of the positive things that occurred during my last game was: Our defensive strategy held the opposing team to 10 points;

2. The second positive thing that occurred during my last game was: Both running backs gained over 100 yards rushing;

3. The third positive thing that occurred during my last game was: Etc.

It is important to also focus on the positive things that occurred during your game because if you only focus on the negative that is all you will see. It reminds me of an old saying I once heard, "You are never as good as you think you are, but you are never as bad either." Looking at both negative and positive elements of your coaching performance just gives you a more balanced perspective on what's really going on for you.

As you can clearly see, the HK Journaling exercise allows you to document a tremendous amount of information regarding your coaching performance, and the problems that came up for you. If you called a bad play during a crucial point in the game, something motivated you to do that. And, that something was mental, and that is what we want to clear using this process.

Now, let's discuss how the HK Performance Trigger is used to clear the information that surfaced for you during your HK Journaling exercise.

Mastering The Mental Side Of Coaching

How To Use The HK Performance Trigger

With the onion analogy I explained that the center of the onion represents the winning coach you have the potential to become. The layers of mental blockages in the form of synthesizing events that you have accumulated over the years are responsible for preventing you from becoming that coach.

What's creating problems with your coaching right now is the fact that you carry these mental blockages with you from game to game. It's as if you are walking through a mental revolving door. I suggest that you do the HK Journaling the evening after each and every game in which you coach.

What follows is a four step process that will allow you to peel away the layers of mental blockages responsible for creating the problems you are now experiencing with your coaching:

Step #1: If you haven't already, go back to the chapter on Programming In The HK Performance Trigger. Program in the trigger by following Steps 1 through 3 (Once the trigger is programmed in you never have to do it again);

Step #2: Read your HK Journaling list starting with the negative things that came up for you during your coaching performance and read them one at a time;

Step #3: After reading the first item on the negative side of your list, hit your trigger. Say or mentally state the word "relax" and touch the thumb and index fingers of both hands, and open them. Move to the second negative thing and do the same thing until you have gone through the entire negative list;

Step #4: Now, move to the positive list and repeat Step #3 until you have gone through the entire positive list;

This is extremely effective because your Subconscious Mind stored every aspect of your coaching performance earlier that day. Doing the HK Journaling exercise allows you to access that information from your Subconscious Mind and any mental blockages attached to it.

Using the HK Performance Trigger creates a medium whereby you can clear and release those synthesizing events so that you don't carry them with you into your next game. Here's why this is so effective. Suppose one of the negative things that came up for you during your post game HK Journaling was that you make a bad call during a crucial point in the game that adversely affected the outcome.

When you read that statement, your Conscious Mind will send instructions to your Subconscious Mind, "Send up all the information you have in storage relating to the bad call I made in our game earlier today."

When that information comes up from your Subconscious Mind, it will bring all the mental blockages (synthesizing events) associated with it as well. When you hit your HK Performance Trigger, it allows you to subconsciously neutralize and clear away yet another layer of this mental onion that has grown around your coaching.

My suggestion is to punch holes in the completed exercises and keep them in a three ring binder. Once a month or so, review them and see if you can find

Mastering The Mental Side Of Coaching

any patterns that may be developing in your coaching that may need addressing.

In fact, the question you should be asking yourself after each game is, "What could I have done to improve my coaching during this game?" If you don't think this process is effective, Byron Nelson, a former PGA Tour player, won 18 tournaments in one year (11 in a row!) back in the 1940's doing the exact same thing. If it worked for him, it will certainly work for you.

Mind Mastery For Coaching

Mastering The Mental Side Of Coaching

I created program for coaches called *Mind Mastery For Coaching*. It includes the DVD *Change Your Thinking, Change Your Life*, and a powerful 30 minute CD titled *Becoming A Winning Coach*. The DVD explains HK and how I use muscle testing when working with individuals to help them clear blockages preventing them from successfully accomplishing their goals.

The CD is designed and intended to work on a subconscious level and can be used as a pre-game mental preparation regimen that will put you in a mental space that will allow you to coach your best during the game. The same HK Trigger word (relax) is programmed in at the beginning of the CD.

The CD contains over 100 statements relating specifically to coaching and winning. Each statement is followed by the trigger word relax. For instance, one of the statements on the CD is, "Release all fear from your mind and body preventing you from becoming a winning coach." This statement, and all statements on the CD, are followed by the trigger word relax.

Any subconsciously stored fear relating to the statement will surface, and the trigger word relax is simply a medium that will allow you to neutralize and subconsciously release it. The reason it works is because "Energy Follows Intention!" Repeated listening to the CD will help you peel away layers of mental blockages from this subconscious onion you have created over the years preventing you from becoming a winning coach.

Here is what you do. One to two hours before game time, find a quiet location to sit or recline. Close your eyes and do your best to consciously listen to each statement. Pay close attention to any physiological changes or sensations you may experience in your body after hearing the trigger word relax. You may find yourself taking a deep breath or yawning. This simply means that a very subtle energy shift is occurring for you on a subconscious level relating to one of the statements you just heard on the CD.

It is recommended that you listen to the CD before and after each game. The CD is designed to work on a subconscious level because that is where your coaching problems are. Listening to the CD before your games helps you to mentally prepare by clearing out the cobwebs. Listening to the CD after your games helps to peel away layers of mental blockages that may have surfaced for you during your coaching performance.

Think of your age. That's how old your belief system is. If for instance, you can only win 10% of the games you coach, it is simply your belief system acting out through your physical body. And, it will perpetuate your low win/loss percentage. Listening to the CD daily allows you to peel away the layers of this onion manifesting for you as a 10% win/loss ratio.

Remember that when stress is present in your body it will also cause one or both hemispheres of your brain to weaken or switch off. It is when the brain is in this weakened state that the sabotaging anomaly will manifest for you.

Listening to the CD coupled with the HK Journaling will provide you with an excellent regimen to help you accelerate the peeling away of the layers of negative information preventing you from reaching your true potential to become a winning coach.

I cannot stress the important of listening to the CD before and after each game. Even after practice. Sometimes it is difficult for you to take 30 minutes out of your day to sit down and listen to the CD. If this is the case, I suggest that you buy a small portable CD player and place it at the head of you bed. Turn it on before you drift off to sleep with the volume low.

Although the best results will be achieved from listening to the CD while in your waking conscious state, you will still derive substantial benefits from listening to it as you drift off to sleep. Listening to the CD allows you to do everything in your power to become mentally prepared for your upcoming game. You may also listen to the CD while driving in your car; jogging, etc. Listening to the CD accelerates the removal of the layers of blockages preventing you from become a winning coach.

Setting Goals

After Tiger Woods won his first Masters, he skipped a tournament, and came back and won the next tournament. During his post tournament interview, he was asked why he thought he won the tournament. Tiger Woods looked at the interviewer surprisingly and replied, "Because it was my goal to win it."

How does your physical body know what your mind expects from it if you do not set a goal? I hate to use cliques, but this one is so appropriate. When you don't set goals, it is like a ship without a rudder. It just spins in circles. ALWAYS SET GOALS!

I suggest that you set a goal before each competition. Here's what you do. The night before your game, grab a pencil and paper and write down your goal. After documenting your goal, read it aloud and use your HK Performance Trigger to clear. Let's assume you are a basketball coach. Here is how you would set your goal.

Example:

Step #1: I, (coach's name,) now choose to win our game against (opponent's name), and I will do my best to help my team win by coaching to the best of my ability, and I will do my best to make those decisions during the game that will allow our team to emerge victorious. I will motivate and inspire my players to play their best and win the game. I will remain calm, relaxed and focused on my goal to win the game. This or something better;

Step #2: Hit your HK Performance Trigger by stating or thinking the word "relax" and touching the thumb and index fingers of both hands, and opening them;

Mastering The Mental Side Of Coaching

Step #3: Read your goal aloud again.

You may modify the language to suit your particular sport. Repeating this process before every game allows your mind an opportunity to communicate your intentions to your physical body that your goal is to help coach your team so that they win the game.

Now, if you do not achieve a victory in your game, it simply means that your mental onion needs additional peeling. You still have mental blockages that need to be cleared. Please do your best to remain objective during this process.

Doing the HK Journaling, setting goals and listening to the CD will help you on the road to becoming a winning coach by peeling away the layers of mental blockages stopping you from realizing your goal.

In fact, before you run out to the court, or onto the field, so that your players can take their warm-ups, every player on your team should set a goal to win the game. The reason this is so powerful is that it allows every player to verbalize the team goal to win the game, but it also puts every team player on the same page. And, that is, or should be, to win the game.

ALWAYS SET A GOAL TO WIN THE GAME!

Your Athlete's Mechanics

It's very important to understand what happens hemispherically to your player's when they are executing the mechanics of their sport during game situations. At some point in their athletic development, every player was shown how to correctly execute the mechanics of their particular sport.

That information was stored somewhere in their Subconscious Mind(s). What prevents your players from accessing that mechanical information during actual game situations is stress. Earlier I had mentioned that when there is stress present in an athlete's body that stress causes one or both hemispheres of his brain to weaken or switch off.

I have other Mind Mastery programs and books relating the mental side of golf, tennis, pitching, hitting, basketball, football, soccer, winning and learning that may help players understand why they are struggling with consistency during competition. They are available at www.hk-relax.com and amazon.com.

This switching off phenomenon affects his thought processes as well as the correct mechanical execution relative to his particular sport. And it affects athletes who compete individually as well as athletes who compete on teams.

When stress is present in an athlete's physical body, it causes his body to weaken. When his body is in this weakened state, he will drop a pass thrown right into his hands in the end zone that may have won the football game, or miss two free throws with one second left that might have won the basketball game. The presence of stress in the player's physical body is so pervasive that it hampers and dramatically affects both the mental and mechanical functioning of his body. This is the anomaly responsible for adversely altering his play, and will cause him to make uncharacteristic mental or mechanical errors at crucial moments during the game. Here's why.

The right hemisphere of the player's brain controls the left side of his physical body, while the left hemisphere of his brain controls the right side. Let's assume you player's sport is basketball. When his right hemisphere weakens or switches off during his shot making during a game, it weakens the left side of his physical body.

When he takes a shot during a game with a weak left side, it dramatically alters the mechanical dynamics of that particular shot and will cause him to miss. There is no way he can consistently play his best with his body in this weakened state. This weakened state is so subtle it cannot be seen with the naked eye, and that is where muscle testing comes in.

This switching off phenomenon not only affects him physically, but mentally as well. For instance, if a basketball player is in his left hemisphere when playing a game, he will have a tendency to play conservatively and may pass the ball rather than take an open shot. Conversely, if the player is in his right hemisphere he will take a low percentage shot rather than pass to an open man. You can see how this phenomenon can adversely affect your player's continuity during competition.

How do you get your player's to play their hearts out for you and give their all during games? You do it by gaining their respect. You do it by understanding how your players react to certain things that you say and do while communicating with them.

Communicating With Your Athletes

All people basically want is to be validated. The same holds true when communicating. When you see two people arguing, all they are doing is invalidating what the other person is saying. Webster's defines communication as, "a. A giving or exchanging of information; b. To have a sympathetic or meaningful relationship."

Please note that the words exchanging and sympathetic are used in the definition. In order for communication to occur there must be reciprocity. And, that means there must be a mutual exchange of information. One of the best books I have found on communication and one that I highly recommend to people with whom I work is a book titled "How To Talk So Kids Will Listen, And Listen So Kids Will Talk" by Adele Faber & Elaine Mazlish.

Don't let the title fool you. Let me show you how simple it is. Let's assume you are a basketball coach and you are playing an actual game and you called time and one of your players is very upset and has come to you during the time out and says, "Coach that Johnson keeps fouling me and the ref won't call it!"

Now, there is one of two ways you can answer your player's complaint. One response will validate what he is saying and feeling while the other response will invalidate what he is saying or feeling. If you respond to your player with something like, "Reynolds, don't be such a crybaby, and suck it up," you have just invalidated what your player was saying and feeling.

Your response basically told him that what he was saying or feeling was wrong. Reynolds will feel invalidated and it will make him angry. An angry player will not perform well because the anger will weaken or switch off one hemisphere of his brain. With one hemisphere switched off his effectiveness on the court will become severely compromised.

If you responded to your player with something like, "Reynolds, I can see that you are very upset, but in spite of what Johnson is doing to you we are still going to have to find a way to win this game, OK?" Notice how different this response feels. Instead of Reynolds becoming imbued with anger and all its ramifications you've just validated what he was saying and feeling, and now he can move on.

I have seen and heard coaches who humiliate and speak very condescendingly to their players in front of others. If you read the chapter on the Egocentric Stage again you will understand why speaking like that to someone will never engender respect. It will instead produce resentment on the player's part, and a resentful player will never perform to his potential during competition.

Most psychologists spend 95% of their session with their clients just listening to them. They know if they can let their clients get whatever it is that's bothering them off their chests and tell it to someone who will validate what they are saying and feeling the session will be a success.

I entreat you to read and use the techniques in this wonderful book (How To Talk So Kids Will Listen And Listen So Kids Will Talk) and I guarantee that you will gain an understanding about supportively communicating with your players and they will surely reciprocate by playing their hearts out for you.

Using Imagination During Practice

Imagination is defined as, "The action or faculty of forming mental images or concepts of what is not actually present to the senses." When you imagine yourself doing something, you are going to subconsciously access the same information as if you were physically doing it. Using imagination during practice is extremely effective because it has a twofold benefit.

First, since imagination is located in the right hemisphere of your player's brain, every time they use it they are exercising that part of their brains. If you can keep the right hemisphere of your player's brains switched on during your practice sessions, chances are you will keep them switched on during the actual game.

Secondly, your Subconscious Mind cannot distinguish between something real or imagined. If you don't believe me try telling someone who has a fear of heights that they have nothing to be afraid of. You will fail miserably. That's because the thought of going near a high place creates so much stress in the individual's body that they do not even want to go there mentally.

To get the most out of your team practices use imagination by having your starters play a scrimmage with your non-starting players. Have your non-starting players assume the roles of your next opponent. Be certain that everyone who is playing is aware of it. For instance, if it's a football scrimmage, have the offense assume the role of your next opponent. Here is why this is so effective.

Remember earlier we stated that when you engage in a particular activity your Conscious Mind sends instructions to your Subconscious Mind, i.e., "Send me all the information you have stored in your memory banks relating to this activity?" The stored information your player's access will dictate how well or how poorly they perform.

When your players use their imagination during practice they will access the same subconsciously stored information that they would use if they were really doing whatever it is that they are imagining. They may consciously think they are not playing a real game, but they will be subconsciously. Now, what happens the next day when they are really playing their next opponent is their subconscious minds will think, "Been here and done that, or this seems really familiar."

Observing your players in this practice scenario allows you to determine how that player will perform subconsciously during the real game. If, for instance, your field goal kicker missed a 36 year field goal with 5 seconds on the clock during your last game, during your next practice have your field goal kicker imagine a real game situation and that there are 5 seconds left on the clock and he has to kick a 36 yard field goal. Have him keep kicking until he makes 5 in a row. This imagination scenario can be done with any sport.

Imagination is so effective that during the final round of the 1994 United States Women's Open Golf Championships, Lauri Merten was on the practice putting green imagining herself putting to win the tournament. Four hours later she was hoisting the trophy as the 1994 United States Women's Golf Open champion. Imagination is a very powerful and effective tool, and it works. I entreat you to integrate imagination into your practice regime.

Conclusion

It is said that "Adversity introduces a man to himself." It is my wish that when you encounter adversity during the course of your coaching experiences, that you will not only know where it came from, but be able to constructively deal with it using HK and the disciplines outlined in this book.

I don't specifically know what you are going to have to do to become a winning coach, but on some level of your awareness you do. Using this program faithfully will help you peel away those mental blockages preventing you from accessing that information so that you can realize your goal of becoming a winning coach.

To gain the maximum benefit from this program it is important to use the entire program, which entails:

- Programming in the HK Trigger;
- Faithfully using HK Journaling after each game by documenting negative and positive information relating to your coaching performance;
- Listening to the CD "Becoming A Winning Coach" before and after each game.
- Always set a goal to win!

In closing, please remember that we are dealing with a tremendous amount of information in your subconscious mind relating to your coaching career that has been stored over a period of many years. Please do your best to remain objective while using this program.

I trust that I have given you a perspective that will allow you to more fully understand how your Mind influences your performance as a coach. And, that I have provided you with a remedy that can accelerate positive changes for you that will help you achieve peak performance, not only during your coaching experiences, but ultimately improve the quality of your personal life as well.

A wise man wrote years ago that we can't be Batman to all the Robins in the world. You cannot control what other people think or feel about you, but you can control what you think and feel about yourself. Please remember that coaching, like life, is relative, and that among the blind, the one eyed man is King. "Relax."

***

HK Mind Mastery Programs:

Mind Mastery For Golf
Mind Mastery For Soccer
Mind Mastery For Tennis
Mind Mastery For Hitting
Mind Mastery For Winning
Mind Mastery For Pitching
Mind Mastery For Coaching
Mind Mastery For Basketball
Mind Mastery For Money
Mind Mastery For Selling
Mind Mastery For Learning
Mind Mastery For Peace of Mind
Mind Mastery For Weight Loss
Change Your Thinking Change Your Life (DVD)

Other books by Ernest Solivan:

Quantum Psychophysics (A Treatise on HK)
Mastering The Mental Side of Soccer
Mastering The Mental Side of Tennis
Mastering The Mental Side of Hitting
Mastering The Mental Side of Football
Mastering The Mental Side of Pitching
Mastering The Mental Side of Winning
Mastering The Mental Side of Coaching
Mastering The Mental Side of Basketball
Mastering The Mental Side of Putting
Mastering The Mental Side of Tournament Golf
Pro Se Cites & Authorities

For more information about HK contact:
Performance Consultants International
Website: www.hk-relax.com

www.ingramcontent.com/pod-product-compliance
Lightning Source LLC
Chambersburg PA
CBHW021016090426
42738CB00007B/800